T0088337

RUBANK
Elementary
METHOD

CELLO

SYLVAN D. WARD

A FUNDAMENTAL COURSE FOR INDIVIDUAL
OR LIKE-INSTRUMENT CLASS INSTRUCTION

RUBANK®

HAL•LEONARD®

How to Hold the Cello and Bow

The correct position for holding the instrument and bow is very important in beginning the study of the Cello. The illustrations given here will guide you in holding your instrument correctly. Refer to them often when you are practicing at home so you will not get into bad habits which are later hard to overcome.

Illustration 1.

Sit up straight. Fit the cello between your legs so it feels firm and comfortable. Rest the upper part of the cello lightly against your chest. Adjust the end pin so the instrument is at the right elevation to allow your bow to move freely over the strings without bumping into your leg. The right elevation is usually obtained when the lowest tuning peg comes just opposite the left ear lobe.

Illustration 2.

Shows the position of the thumb resting lightly on the back of the neck in under the fingers. The tendency of the thumb is to be under the 2nd finger moreso than indicated in the illustration. Take position similar to that of holding a ball. Notice also how the fingers are rounded out over the strings, and that the joints of the fingers do not cave in.

Illustration 3.

Shows the manner of holding the bow in the right hand. Notice especially the curved position of the thumb.

Learning To Bow On The Open Strings

The exercises on this page are to enable you to get the "feel" of the bow, and draw it straight (parallel with the bridge.) Note values and counting will be taken up on the next page.

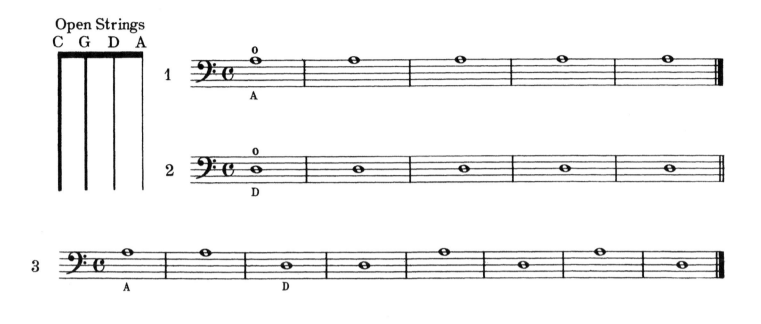

Check up on the way you are holding the bow.
Are you curving your thumb correctly?

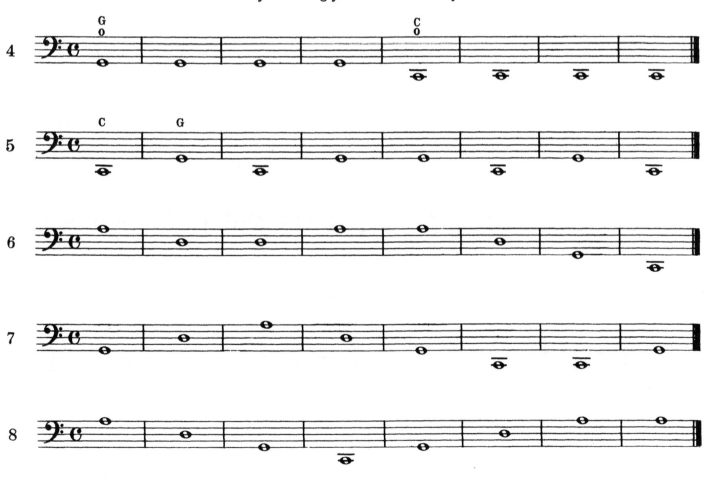

Copyright MCMXXXVI by Rubank, Inc., Chicago
International Copyright Secured

38854-48

Half Notes and Half Rests

Quarter Notes
(Count one beat to each)

Use most of the bow, but draw it straight.

Quarter Rest – 𝄽

M (means to play in the middle portion of your bow.)

Whole Notes and Whole Rests

Using the Half Notes, Quarter Notes and Whole Notes Together

Using the First Finger

Place the first finger down approximately three inches from the end of the fingerboard.

1

2

3
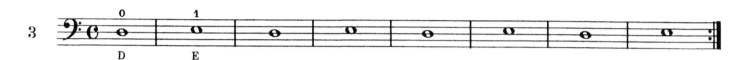

4

5

6

7

8

9

10

11

38854

Using the Third Finger

Some teachers prefer to introduce the 2nd finger before the 3rd finger. If so turn to page 11.

Melody

Finger Play

S. D. W.

March

S. D. W.

NOTE: In learning the first three notes of the scale in which you use the open string, first and third fingers, it is desirable to first sing the three notes with Do, Re, Mi before playing them. This will help finger placement and intonation. Of course the voice will be sounding at least an octave higher than the pitch of the instrument.

Third Finger on the D String

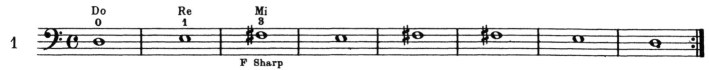

Notice the F Sharp has been put here (in the signature) which means that all F's in this little solo will be called F sharp.

Little Solo

S. D. W.

Third Finger on the A String

The C sharp has been put in the signature, so all the C's in this piece will be called C sharp.

Dotted Half Notes

A dot increases the value of a note one half.

Watch the sharps

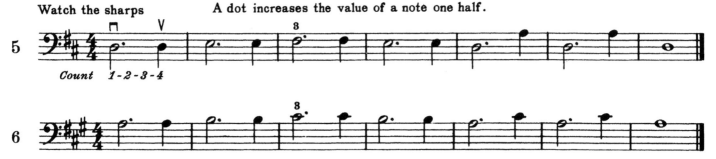

Count 1 - 2 - 3 - 4

Adding the Fourth Finger

Half step between the 3rd and 4th fingers

Familiar Melody on the G String

Melody on the C String

Melody on the A String

S.D.W.

Largo

DVORAK

Using the Second Finger

A Little Exercise

C MAJOR SCALE

Staccato

Keep the bow on the string – Move it quickly – Stop it quickly

Our Old Clock

S. D. W.

Alla Breve Time

Quickens the time. Means each half note gets one beat.

March Cadet

S. D. W.

The Second Finger on the G String

F MAJOR SCALE

6/8 Time

M.

Count 1 - 2 - 3 - 4 - 5 - 6

March Away

S. D. W.

Count 1 - 2 - 3 - 4-5-6

Lullaby

S. D. W.

p

Stop the bow slightly for
the quarter note.

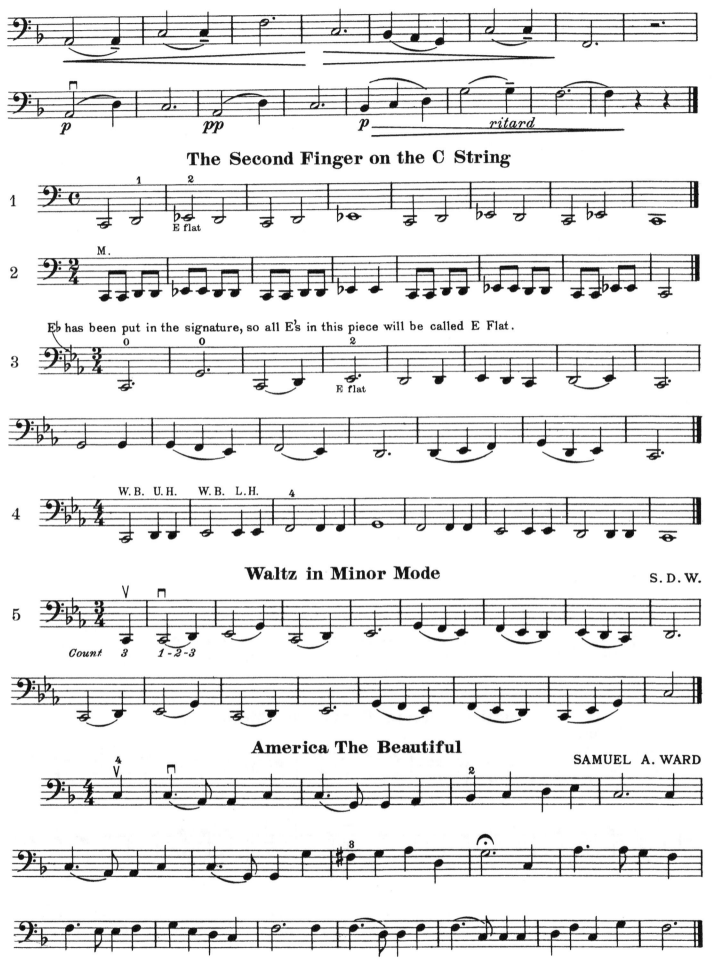

The Second Finger on the C String

Waltz in Minor Mode
S. D. W.

America The Beautiful
SAMUEL A. WARD

Eb has been put in the signature, so all E's in this piece will be called E Flat.

Bowing 2 Strings At One Time
(DOUBLE STOPS)

She'll Be Comin' 'Round The Mountain

Lively

Bowing Exercises

Pt. (means at the point of the bow)
Fr. (means at the frog)

Move the bow lightly

Wrist Bowing

Practice slowly at first
then increase tempo.

Play like preceding measure

Play like preceding measure

Bowing in Style

S. D. W.

First time play at the point

Second time play at the frog

38854

Stretch Exercises

Rule: Where you have 2 consecutive whole steps you use the 1-2-4 combination of fingering instead of 1-3-4.

F Sharp - Notice it is in the signature

Keep the fingers down on the C string while playing the open G.

C Sharp

Fingering Exercise in "A" Major

A MAJOR SCALE — Lift fingers only when necessary.

Variations on the Scale

Singing Strings

S. D. W.

Fun With Intervals

Also practice lower fingering.

1

2 Look at signature.

Fr.

Start and Stop

Stop the bow for each staccato note.

3

Count   and   1 and 2 and 3 and 4 and

Abide With Me

WILLIAM H. MONK

Half step
D Sharp

This is called a "Natural" and means to cancel the sharp.

Broadly

Fingering Exercises in B♭ Major

Preparation for B♭ Major Scale

B♭ MAJOR SCALE — Practice the scale with different bowings and rhythms.

Sixteenth Notes

Variation on B♭ Major Scale

Dotted Eighth Notes

Oh! Susanna

STEPHEN C. FOSTER

Count   and   1 and 2 and

Drink To Me Only With Thine Eyes

OLD ENGLISH

Playing Triplets

Watch fingering. Your half steps and whole steps decide which fingering to use.

Accents

Practice different bowings

Etude

Watch your fingering

S. D. W.

Practice with and without the accents on the quarter notes.

etc.

Pizzicato (Plucking the Strings)

Pluck the string with the forefinger of the right hand, allowing the bow to rest against the palm with the hair turned away from the string. Place the thumb down on the edge of the fingerboard near the C string.

Amaryllis Gavotte

KING LOUIS XIII

Jingle Bells

J. PIERPONT

Count 1 and 2 and 3 and 4 and

Etude

S. D. W.

38854

Second Position *

Up to here you have been playing in the first position. In order to play higher notes on the "A" string it is necessary to play in other positions. This book takes up the first four and one half positions. In shifting from first to second position, merely slide the thumb and fingers quickly up the neck of the instrument.

Remember, the thumb touches the neck of the Cello very lightly.

* If the teacher prefers to take up the third position, or the fourth position before the second, this may be done.

Shifting to Second Position (Continued)

Crossing the Strings in Position

Third Position

Melody

Exercise

Is your left thumb relaxed?

Nowell

Play fingering as marked for practice

TRADITIONAL

Shifting Directly from 1st to 3rd Position

Shifting Directly to 3rd Position (Continued)

All Through The Night

WELSH AIR

F Major Scale

Practice scale in different rhythm:
and with various bowings.

Crossing the String

America

HENRY CAREY

D String

Little Etude

S. D. W.

38854

Fourth Position

Scale and Variation

In The Gloaming

ANNIE F. HARRISON

Exercise in Shifting

38854

Old Kentucky Home

STEPHEN C. FOSTER

Slowly

IV

Shift silently

III   IV

Are you shifting smoothly?

IV

II   D String   IV

D String   G String

G String   C String

Crossing the Strings in 4th Position

Dream of Love

FRANZ LISZT

Learning the Trill

Half Position

Exercise in E Minor

Chromatic Waltz

S. D. W.

Scales

Practice with different bowings and in various rhythms.

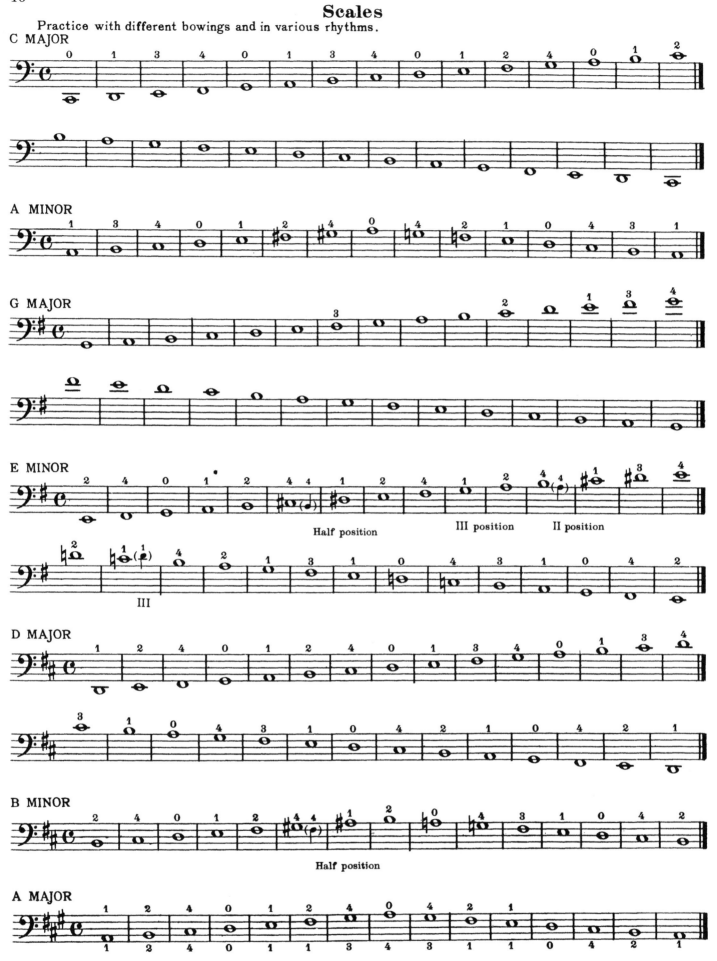

NOTE: The small notes in parenthesis are position guides and are not to be played.

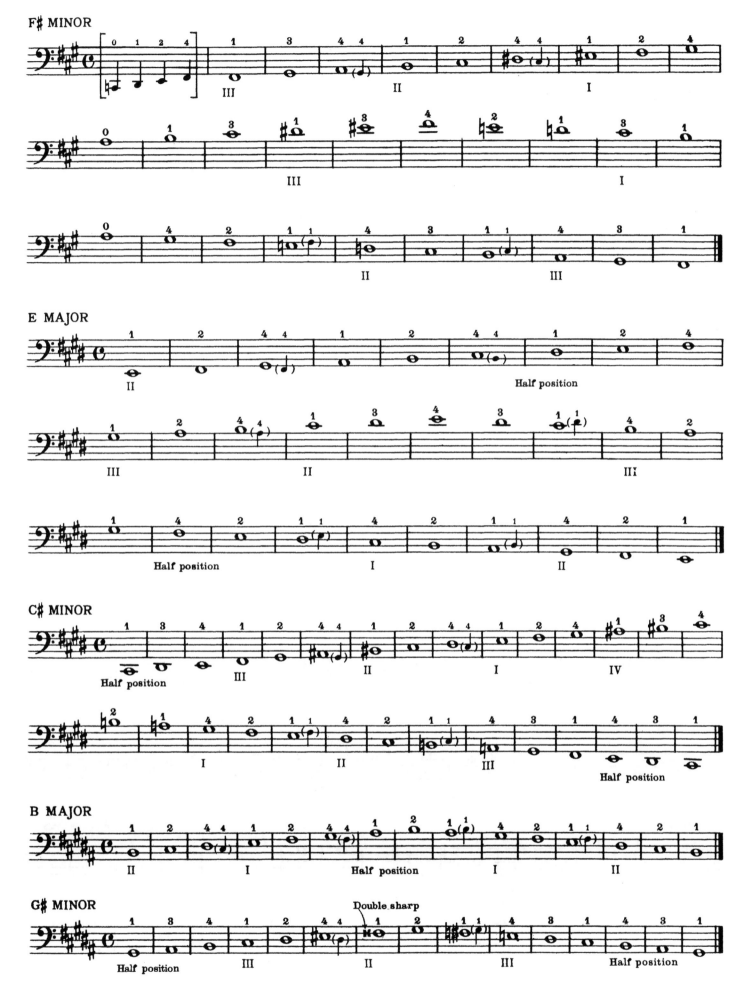

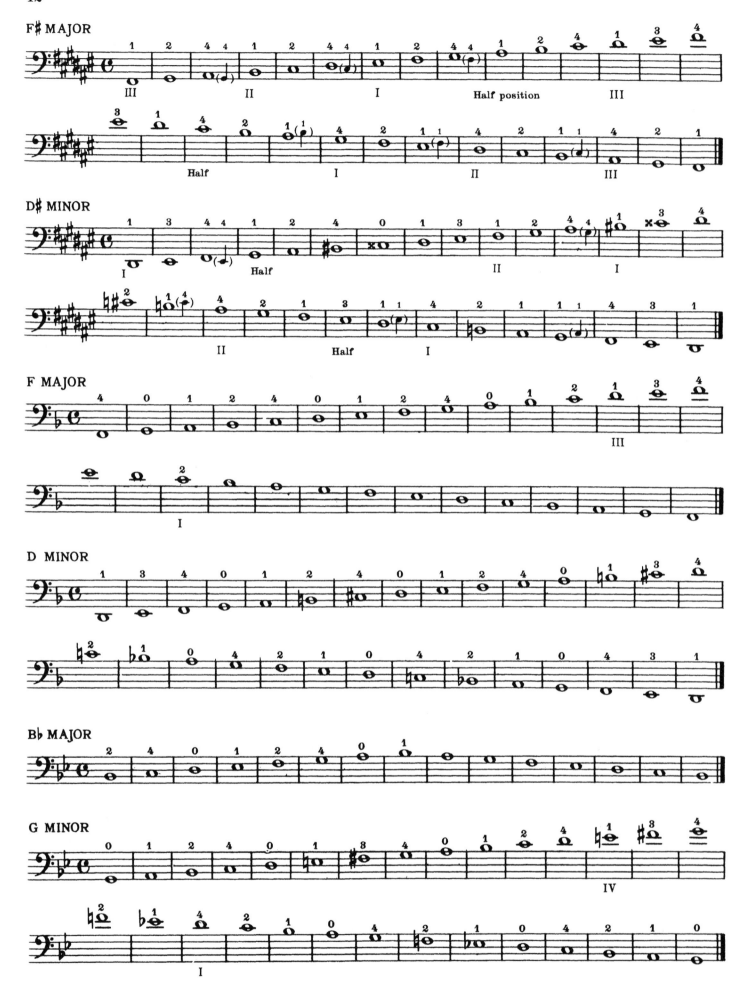

F♯ MAJOR

D♯ MINOR

F MAJOR

D MINOR

B♭ MAJOR

G MINOR

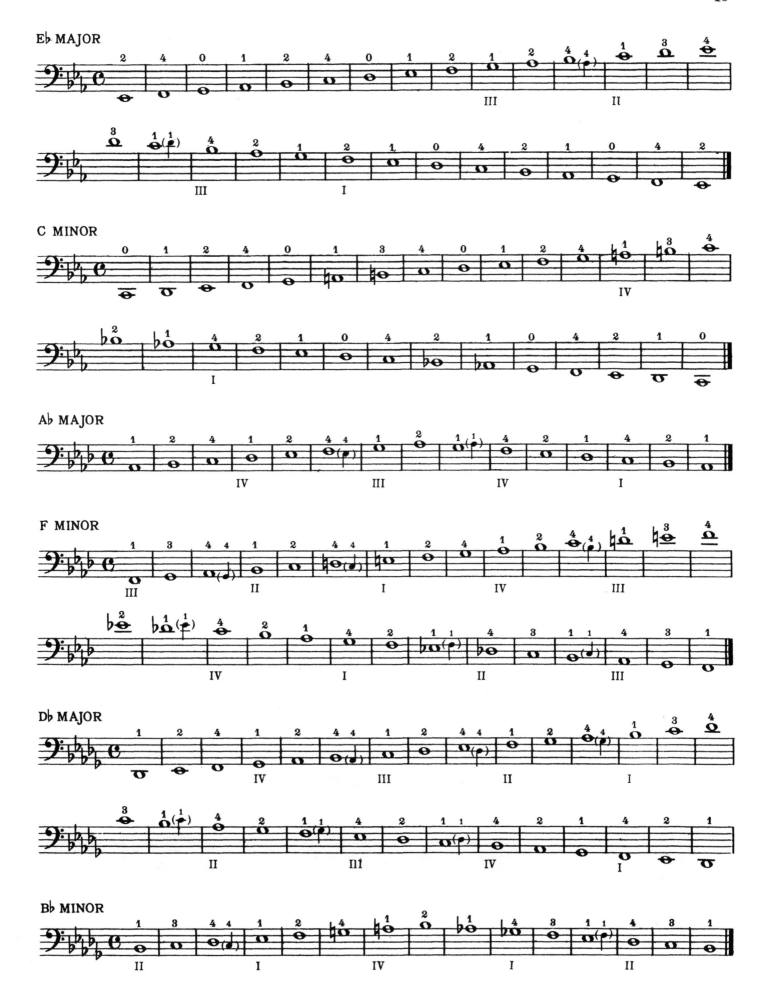

Brahm's Lullaby
(Duet)

Row, Row, Row Your Boat
(Round for 2, 3 or 4 Cellos)

O Sole Mio
(Duet)

Silent Night

FRANZ GRÜBER

Whispering Hope
(Duet)

ALICE HAWTHORNE

Andante moderato

I'll Take You Home Again Kathleen
(Trio)

THOMAS P. WESTENDORF

Reference Chart of 4½ Positions*

Half Position	1st Position	2nd Position	Third Position	Fourth Position

(A String, D String, G String, C String — musical notation chart)

General rule: Where two consecutive whole steps appear, use the 1st, 2nd and 4th fingers for example:

etc.

38854